Walk in Wisdom:
Living Life as God Intended

Stan E. DeKoven

Walk in Wisdom:
Living Life as God Intended

Stan E. DeKoven

Copyright © 2014 Stan E. DeKoven
ISBN 978-1-61529-148-9

Vision Publishing
1672 Main St., E109
Ramona, CA 92065
1-800-9-VISION
www.booksbyvision.com

All rights in this book are reserved worldwide.

No part of the book may be reproduced in any manner whatsoever without written permission of the author except in brief quotations embodied in critical articles of review.

Table of Contents

Introduction 5
Chapter 1: Living Life As God Intended – by Intention 9
Chapter 2: Guidance for the Journey of Life 19
Chapter 3: Identity — Who We Are 35
Chapter 4: Living Life in the Wisdom of God
    by Intention with Discipline 41
Chapter 5: Walk in Wisdom: Choose the Right Gate 47
Addendum 51

Introduction

In the providence of God, I gave up local church pastoring for a teaching ministry. I love preaching and teaching and enjoyed most of pastoring. Although I was relatively good at administration and trained as a counselor, the joy of pastoring was diminished by the pressure of growth, the frustration of finances, and especially by the pain of politics. Of course, in the "larger" arena of educational ministry, there are many political minefields and most seem benign to the raucousness of church conflicts.

Thus, I appreciate so greatly the tremendous work that so many pastors do. Often unheralded and certainly underappreciated, not to mention underpaid, I am honored to work with man. At my best, I serve as a "father" to some, more Uncle Stan to most, while endeavoring to come alongside them to hold up their (at times) weary hands, as co-laborers in the vineyard to which they have been called. Although never perfect, my hope is that I have been more help than hindrance.

"Walk In Wisdom" is based upon the 2013 sermon series preached at the Fontana Christian Center International Ministries, in Fontana, CA, at the church of my dear friends Pastor Gary and Gina Holley. In this small book, my focus is to provide some insight into the important topic of wisdom. In both the preaching and the writing, my intent is to develop both the theological and practical (you must know wisdom, and what wisdom is, before one can walk it out in daily living) aspects of this important biblical concept. I believe a thorough reading of this work will likely help my friends, the pastors, and their beloved, problematic, parishioners grow in the grace and knowledge of our Lord and Savior Jesus Christ. My hope is that you will enjoy this work and be challenged by it. Avail yourself of the free iPod teaching and study guide by yours truly. If you wish to receive these resources, call 1 800 – 9 – VISION or contact ksmith@vision.edu.)

May the Lord bless you as you journey further into the wisdom of God.

Dr. Stan DeKoven

8

Chapter 1:

Living Life As God Intended – by Intention

I had a thought the other day. I know that it could have been caused by bad pizza, but it seemed profound to me. Here it goes...

The ability to do all that we are capable of doing is wrapped up in our DNA from the time of conception. Of course, this does not guarantee that we will achieve our fullest potential, and who is to judge that but God? In similar fashion, the ability to be all that we can be in Christ is already in us by virtue of the DNA of God (Christ in us, the hope of glory; the Holy Spirit living in us). To achieve the fullness of God's intended plan for us is not determined by an accident of birth, but requires our acknowledgement (awareness) of the fact that we are truly a new creation in Christ. We can be and do all that he desires us to be and do through him; *if* we have the correct guidance in what is healthy and appropriate action, develop strong discipline, make a conscious effort at good choices and maintain loving relationships in spite of failures along the way (inevitable consequences of living). In other words, living life fully requires wisdom!

A Simple Testimony

Shortly after I opened my heart to the Lord at age 12, I met with my Pastor Lee Speakman. He instructed me to develop some disciplines that would become lifelong pursuits. He stated that in order to grow in one's faith, there were four primary building blocks requiring daily attention; reading the word of God, prayer, fellowship and witnessing. I took these concepts to heart and began diligently and consistently to lay these building blocks down in my life.

The book of the bible that intrigued me the most was the book of Proverbs. I heard a sermon on the prayer of Solomon. He asked the Lord for wisdom rather than riches and power, it was a prayer gladly granted by the Lord. After hearing this message, I too prayed the prayer of Solomon. Following Solomon's early example, I pursued God with the hope of avoiding his later lifestyle by learning to practice what I would eventually preach, while enjoying the blessings of God (see Ecclesiastes 3).

Well, I wish I could say I avoided the follies of youth based solely on my prayer, but I made my fair share of blunders. Yet, by the grace of God, I have learned a few things and have gained an appreciation for the simple act of submitting to the word of God. Developing a proper understanding of the word helped me to avoid early folly.

What is Wisdom?

Wisdom is defined as the quality of being wise; knowledge, and the capacity to make due use of it; knowledge of the best ends and the best means; discernment and judgment; discretion, sagacity (the quality of being discerning, sound in judgment, and farsighted), skill; dexterity.

I define wisdom from a biblical perspective, for the bible states that the fear of the Lord is the beginning of wisdom and understanding, and we must seek it (see Proverbs 3:13-14; 4:7; 15:14…). Thus, from a biblical perspective wisdom is knowledge, or the accumulation of truth. This leads to understanding, or the "I know what to do," added to application or activation = I do what I can and should do, or I live by faith in God and his word. Another way to state this is that wisdom is to do what God wants, which is generally revealed in the word of God, and more specifically revealed as we walk in daily faith, led by the Holy Spirit. It is not one or the other, either the word or the Spirit; but it is both the word and the Spirit. Both the word and the Spirit are needed to live the Christian life fully and joyfully. In the addendum at the end of this work, you will find an expanded definition of wisdom for those wanting to do deeper study.

Manifold Wisdom

Paul the apostle wrote in Ephesians 3:10-11,

> "…so that through the church the manifold wisdom of God might now be made known to the rulers and authorities in the heavenly places. This was according to the eternal purpose that he has realized in Christ Jesus our Lord."

Living in the manifold wisdom of God can mean that all of the inhabitants of heaven and earth, principalities and powers, workers of darkness, angels and demons, and all of the folks in between can be absolutely assured that Jesus is wisdom, and he has provided his wisdom to live life fully and completely to and through his church. Another view is that the Father, through the Son, empowered by the Holy Spirit, provided the multi-colored wisdom of God and made it accessible to his children. It is as though wisdom can be seen in a colorful display, such as red anger, blue days, green with envy or green pastures, light heartedness, dark days, etc. Of course, the color scheme of God is perfect and pure, not driven by mere emotion, but focused on our benefit and his glory. As we live our lives by God's grace, we manifest God's purposes. Through the Church, we learn wisdom, which is to:

Know him. This means much more than knowing about God. It really means to know his character and his desires for us; beginning with the knowledge that God is good, that he loves us, and has provided us with all that we need for an abundant life.

Trust him. This is a foundational truth that will be expounded upon shortly.

Live life to its fullest, for the glory of God. For all that God has created is for our enjoyment (in moderation, a commonsense principle of wisdom), for again, God is good, all the time, in spite of what life might throw at us.

Trust is the Foundation

> "Proverbs 3:5, 6..."Trust in the Lord with all your heart, and do not lean on what you know, but in everything you do, give God thanks, and he will direct your path."

The very first verse of scripture I memorized after giving my life to Christ was Proverbs 3:5, 6. I suppose the Lord knew that given my background and inclinations, I needed this verse more than others did. It is helpful to remember the steps of the righteous are put in order, or set straight by the Lord himself. So, we must remember:

- Trust is the Key. In any relationship, human or divine, trust is an essential foundation. For how can one develop a relationship between two if one doubts the character or trustworthiness of the person they are relating to? A simple trust in the goodness of God, based upon all he has done for us, is a necessary first step in learning wisdom. The bible states "the fear of the Lord is the beginning of knowledge (the first step in gaining wisdom; you have to know a few things); fools despise wisdom and instruction." Thus, determining in our hearts to fear (trust) in the Lord is an important first step, one which cannot be minimized. Of course, it is not trust alone that matters, but it is…

- Trusting in the Lord, for he is the only one who can be fully trusted. Most of us have been severely disappointed by past relationships, even well meaning, loving people can fail to meet our expectations, legitimate or not. Only the Lord, who never sleeps or slumbers, who is ever watching over us, who cares for us with an eternal and comprehensive love, can be fully trusted to have our backs in every situation, even when we are rebellious or foolish. He is trustworthy. He requires of us as his sons and daughters, that we learn to trust him fully in order to gain the multicolored wisdom of God. Our trust is to be in the Lord, and must flow from our hearts.

- Trust him with all that we have and in all that we have. Our hearts, souls, minds and strength, with our time, talent and treasures, with our hopes and dreams, in our fears and lack, we trust him in everything. This is demonstrated by giving thanks, not for everything, but in every and all circumstances. Of course, this is easier said than done, but it can be done. God would not dangle a promise before us that we had no hope of achieving with his help. Finally,

- Recognize the limitations of our own experience, or the experience of our mamas or daddies. Our friends, family, and even spiritual leaders are all limited in their knowledge and wisdom; especially in regards to the personal life of one of God's uniquely created women or men.

What God promises, he will fulfill, but of course, we must make sure we have clearly heard a promise, knowing it is from him, in a still small voice or from his word; more on this below.

Blessings Follow Because you are Blessed

One of my favorite passages of scripture is found in Romans 8:31-39:

> "What then shall we say to these things? (The reality is that we have been adopted into the family of God, and are now co-heirs with Christ). If God be for us, who can be against us? He who did not spare his own son but gave him up for us all, how will he not also with him graciously give us all things (including, and especially wisdom). Who shall bring any charge against God's elect? It is God who justifies. Who is to condemn? Christ Jesus is the one who died—more than that, who was raised—who is at the right hand of God (and we with him, see Ephesians 2:6), who indeed is interceding for us. Who shall separate us

from the love of Christ? Shall tribulation, or distress, or persecution, famine, or nakedness, or danger, or sword? As it is written 'for your sake we are being killed all the day long; we are regarded as sheep to be slaughtered.' No, in all these things we are more than conquerors through him who loved us. For I am sure that neither death nor life, nor angels nor rulers, nor things present nor things to come, nor powers, nor height nor depth, nor anything else in all creation, will be able to separate us from the Love of God in Christ Jesus our Lord."

We have all blessings already in Christ (Ephesians 1:3), but we must appropriate them, which is done by faith. For example, we have the blessed knowledge of kingdom life, depicted by Paul the apostle as righteousness, peace, and joy in the Holy Spirit. Thus, if we are to have the peace that passes understanding, then we must stand in the knowledge of our right standing in Christ. We are forgiven, cleansed, delivered, and made right; and we must also work to have a right relationship with our spouse, our children, friends, etc. Knowing that we are forgiven and thus righteous before God through Christ is wonderful, but peace will escape us if we are not in a healthy relationship with others (love God, love your neighbor as yourself). Further, we are told, "our God will supply all our needs." (Philippians 4:19). This presupposes that we are generous in heart and wallet, which is difficult if not nearly impossible if we have nothing to give, which is the case if we sit and vegetate rather than working diligently; well I assume you get the point. All blessings are some of the many conditional promises of God. They are conditional based upon a number of things, such as time and chance, and our willingness to cooperate with the principles found in the Word of God.

Wisdom... where art thou?

Chapter 2:

Guidance for the Journey of Life

In many ways, our life is a journey. As described in my book, Journey to Wholeness, we grow in stages. John the apostle in 1 John 2:12-14 lists three stages of spiritual growth, children, young men and fathers. The stages are neither automatic nor guaranteed ...but they are certainly the will of God. We are not to remain as children in immaturity, but we are to grow up to full man and woman hood, which is a process, more than an event. The process of helping someone grow to maturity is called parenting. Thus, I turn your attention to the process or the goal of healthy parenting; it is a part of our walk in wisdom.

The goal of parenting is to prepare the next generation to do more; that is to go farther, be happier and more satisfied with life than we are. Just how do the positive characteristics of healthy parenting manifest in the next generation? It starts with putting first things first.

Patterns and examples from God's Word, advice from biblical sages mixed with practical application that is accepted and acted upon, leads to wisdom. Of course, to create patterns requires examples and an ample amount of time learning the principles of the word of God. It is always best to start young to build healthy traditions. For example, we just completed the Christmas season where the family DeKoven gathered as usual. Along with the gifts and lots of food (too much food), we stopped to read the Christmas story from the gospel of Luke. We prayed and sang happy birthday to Jesus, while remembering that there is no Christmas without Christ. Some would think of that small ritual as quaint, or even boring; but not our family, it is the center of our celebration. These seemingly mundane acts of repeated worship, as we do in local churches every week, are exactly what etch into our grey matter memories that will sustain us when temptations and trials come. My hope is that these simple patterns (and hundreds more) will make an indelible imprint on my grandchildren, as it has on my children, and on and on.

In truth, these patterns in the family help us grapple with what is essential in life, what truly matters? Well, several things come to mind, and it all begins with conception.

Conception is essential. From a most intimate and prayerfully planned encounter, God brings forth life. It is the continuation of God's purpose. From such a small beginning, all of us have come. It may seem as though chance plays a part in our existence. No accident of evolution or mere act of passion caused my children, born in the image of God, to be in our family. The environment of sin and generational iniquities affects us all.

This is true of you as well, for God makes no mistakes. None of us, regardless of the circumstances surrounding our birth, are a mistake or an afterthought. Remember, before the world began he knew us (Jeremiah 1:5). I would add to this several other essential elements, in no specific order. They truly are important to our walk in wisdom. They include…

God our creator is essential. Truly, as I have said in other writings, I do not have enough faith to believe that the world in all its wonder simply happened, that man emerged from some primordial soup. The fool has said in his (or her) heart there is no God….and my mama didn't raise no fool. Simply knowing there is a God is insufficient, the devil knows that only too well. We must learn to...

Fear (honor and respect) the Lord, which is the beginning of knowledge and understanding, leading to wisdom (Proverbs 1:7, 5; 4:7). To fear simply means to show respect for one in authority, one who is greater than you are. Of course, God has all authority, more than any president or celebrity, and He is greater than any world leader or sports hero. If one shows honor and respect to an elected dignitary, or even to a royal, then certainly greater honor and homage belongs to the creator and sustainer of all life.

In our fairly recent movement to make God our friend (which of course he is, for he is the initiator and we the beneficiary), we can become frivolous in our communication with the Lord. A balance needs to be found. This balance is somewhere between boldly coming to his throne and treating Him as a grandpa, and remembering who he is in all of his splendor. "Come, you children, listen to me; I will teach you the fear of the LORD." (Psalms 34:11).

It's All About God...and Us

There is no greater lesson to learn than a genuine awe and respect for God and his creation. How incredible it is to imagine that the God of the universe condescends to hear our voice in prayer and answer us. This baits the question...

How great is God?

Proverbs 6:20-23

> "My son, observe the commandment of your father And do not forsake the teaching of your mother; Bind them continually on your heart; Tie them around your neck. When you walk about, they will guide you; when you sleep, they will watch over you; And when you awake, they will talk to you. For the commandment is a lamp and the teaching is light; And reproofs for discipline are the way of life."

The Word of God alone is proof of the awesomeness of God, as he personally watches over us, guides us, communicates with us and provides the discipline necessary for us to achieve what would be impossible without him, from eternal life to daily bread. God has a wonderful purpose for his children. The prophet Jeremiah echoes this truth in the 29th chapter of Jeremiah, verses 11-13:

> "For I know the plans that I have for you, declares the LORD, plans for welfare and not for calamity to give you a future and a hope. Then you will call upon Me and come and pray to Me, and I will listen to you. You will seek Me and find Me when you search for Me with all your heart."

Of course, we must walk out the plan: Deuteronomy 6:1-9 states:

> "Now this is the commandment, the statutes and the judgments which the LORD your God has commanded me to teach you, that you might do them in the land where you are going over to possess it, so that you and

your son and your grandson might fear the LORD your God, to keep all His statutes and His commandments which I command you, all the days of your life, and that your days may be prolonged...

O Israel, you should listen and be careful to do it, that it may be well with you and that you may multiply greatly, just as the LORD, the God of your fathers, has promised you, in a land flowing with milk and honey. Hear, O Israel! The LORD is our God, the LORD is one! "You shall love the LORD your God with all your heart and with all your soul and with all your might." These words, which I am commanding you today, shall be on your heart. You shall teach them diligently to your sons and shall talk of them when you sit in your house and when you walk by the way and when you lie down and when you rise up. You shall bind them as a sign on your hand and they shall be as frontals on your forehead. You shall write them on the doorposts of your house and on your gates."

The results of living in obedience to the Word of God are seen in Deuteronomy 11:18-28:

"You shall therefore impress these words of mine on your heart and on your soul; and you shall bind them as a sign on your hand, and they shall be as frontals on your forehead. You shall teach them to your sons, talking of them when you sit in your house and when you walk along the road and when you lie down and when you rise up.

You shall write them on the doorposts of your house and on your gates, so that your days and the days of your sons may be multiplied on the land which the LORD swore to your fathers to give them, as long as the heavens remain above the earth.

For if you are careful to keep all this commandment which I am commanding you to do, to love the LORD your God, to walk in all His ways and hold fast to Him, then the LORD will drive out all these nations from before you, and you will dispossess nations greater and mightier than you.

Every place on which the sole of your foot treads shall be yours; your border will be from the wilderness to Lebanon, and from the river, the river Euphrates, as far as the western sea. No man will be able to stand before you; the LORD your God will lay the dread of you and the fear of you on all the land on which you set foot, as He has spoken to you.

See, I am setting before you today a blessing and a curse: the blessing, if you listen to the commandments of the LORD your God, which I am commanding you today; and the curse, if you do not listen to the commandments of the LORD your God, but turn aside from the way which I am commanding you today, by following other gods which you have not known."

God's promise of long life and the possession of His blessed favor (grace) are tied to but not caused by our obedience to God's Word. I know for certain that long term fulfillment, prosperity, joy and eternal destiny are related to a joyful obedience to God's Word.

Love and Fear of the Lord are Linked

Yes, love and fear are linked. Not in the sense of poor parenting where a parent might say to his or her child that I am hitting you because I love you, or I love you, go play on the freeway. God is love, and because it is his very nature, he cannot help but seek the very best for the object of his love; that is, you and me. Because we love him in response to his love, our heart is to worship and adore him, with words and actions. This begins with our respect for the Lord, and our desire to please him, not because he will reject us if we do not, but because we know that no matter what he loves us and provides grace for us.

Learning to accept his love, to trust in his grace, and to walk in his kindness towards the Lord and the world, is part of our maturation process. Thus, from a place of security in his abundant love and acceptance, we seek guidance in all areas of life, and in all relationships of significance. This begins with seeking…

Guidance for Family Life

Family, the very thing God created and desires most, can be problematic at best. Of course, regardless of the family you may have been born into, it was and is just the family God has or will use to mold character, launch purpose, and provide comfort in trouble or trouble for the comfortable. I did not always have this perspective, and you may not either, depending on the level of function or dysfunction you may have experienced. I have decided to believe (more on faith below) that my parents did the best they could, given who they were, their knowledge of parenting, their education in general, personality and temperament, etc. I could focus on negative experiences, but to what gain? They are/were who they are/were, and we are who we are; accept what you cannot change, change what you can.[1]

You will most likely never change your parents or your children for that matter, so give up the vain pursuit, and learn to love and accept, not inappropriate or destructive behavior, but the people in your family as they are. Many of my fondest and funniest moments in life revolve around the fruits, flakes and nuts (of which I am one) in my family. So, if you were blessed with a mom and dad, as God gives you strength, love them.

If you are under 12 years of age, obey them for this is right, and if older, honor them. Speak well of them and do all that you can to respect them, but not necessarily obey. This requires wisdom, for you would be foolish to obey a parent who has little or no expertise in a particular subject. The same applies to your very different siblings. Seeking experts in both knowledge and experience to advise you on issues of life is commendable and recommended, and if a family member happens to have the requisite skills to help

---

[1] Modification of The Serenity Prayer, the common name for an originally untitled prayer by the American theologian Reinhold Niebuhr (1892-1971).

you, give thanks. So, obey as a child, honor as an adult, and in all things...

Love

As stated so eloquently by Dr. Chant in his book, "Christian Life," love has many meanings. For some, it is simply an adjective to most anything they appreciate or admire (I love Taylor Swift, I love my football team, I love pizza, I love my dog, my wife, etc.). There are four primary Greek words for love, with different meanings, and all are important.

Eros speaks of passionate, erotic love, certainly a blessing in a healthy marriage. Second is philia or phileo; a brotherly or sisterly love, friendship, companionship, etc. Again, life is certainly made sweeter when one has friends on the journey of life. Storge speaks of family love, a deeper fidelity than friendship requiring a loyalty to one another that goes beyond friendship.

Thank God for healthy families, even dysfunctional ones. Finally, there is agape, or self-sacrificial love, as is the love of God. Now, all aspects of love are good, and accepting perhaps for agape love, all require a certain amount of wisdom as we express our love and receive love in return. A few examples might be helpful.

Eros is wonderful in marriage, but is not the be all and end all of a healthy marriage. In our highly sexualized culture, it would seem that sex, often and explosive is all that matters in life. Of course, it is important, and the bible speaks against neglecting this experience that is to be shared only between a husband and wife. However, friendship, the building of a family, and sacrifice are also needed in a healthy marriage. Thus, this unique form of communication and communion is important for marital happiness, yet if physical or other issues hindering this expression of love legitimately exist, self-sacrifice is often needed, and becomes an even truer expression of love.

Sir Elton John sang,

> "Making friends for the world to see
> Let the people know you got what you need
> With a friend at hand
> You will see the light
> If your friends are there then everything's all right."

Well, I am not sure that **friends** are that necessary, but they are certainly important. Jesus, after years of living and working with his disciples, told them to call him friend (he seemed to have three special friends, and perhaps John, according to his own telling of the story, was his BFF). Abraham was a friend of God…so friends are important.

Yet, one must be careful with friends, especially if they require more of you in terms of time and energy than you can rightly give, requiring loyalty to an extreme (like me more than anyone, and only like who I like, or I won't be your friend), or have morphed into life style changes that you no longer value. Some friendships are for life, some for a season; some are healthy and we grow with them, some are unhealthy and we hopefully survive and learn from them.

Family is important, and our love for mom and dad, brother and sister, grandma and grandpa, etc. is important. Yet even with family, one must be wise. For not everyone in a family can be trusted equally, loyalty to family can and should be tested against our loyalty to God. Just because mom or dad are to be honored does not mean, especially after age 12, obeyed. In the best of families, we learn to share and care, give and take, laugh and cry.

In the worst of families, we can experience rejection, abandonment, betrayal and even abuse. Thus, family life, like friendships, must be evaluated in the light. This is problematic in dysfunctional, shame-based families that fear that the world will find out that they are not perfect (a delusion of epic proportions). No family is perfect; but it is ours; so love as best you can, forgive often and quickly, and help as God gives strength and ability.

Agape love, sacrificial love, or God like love is by far the most profound, and surprising. To love sacrificially is to look out for the other more than self; to share life out of principle rather than for gain. As humans, we can strive to live in an agape lifestyle. We will no doubt fall short…but strive we must. Sacrificial love will flow out of our transformed character as we identify with our true nature, Christ in us, our hope of glory.

Faith

Faith and trust are virtually synonymous. Having true faith in God is to put your simple trust in his goodness. God is good; all the time, although we don't always feel that he is good, or present, or on our side, but he is. Faith, similar to love, is essential. Trust or faith is the foundation necessary for the building of any relationship. Of course, trust in the Lord, having faith in God's faithfulness, does not take a lot of faith…you either believe God is good or you don't. Putting faith or trust in people, well, that is another thing. Faith in people, institutions, churches, or leaders must be given (at least at first) and then earned; not everyone, or every institution deserves our undying loyalty or faith.

Being cynical but not jaded, especially in the world in which we live, is not a bad place to be. If you will, wisdom says we are to guard our heart, for out of our hearts proceed the issues of life (Proverbs 4:23). Simply stated, our heart (the center of our thoughts and feelings) is tender and it can be easily hurt, and inevitably will be. Thus, we guard our hearts and share our lives only with people that can be trusted; or at least we try. For in truth, there is no human soul that has not been wounded, rejected, abandoned or betrayed at some time in their life, whether it be by friend or foe. Thus, to the best of one's ability, we must guard our hearts. Trust well, have true faith in the goodness of God and the best of mankind, forgive quickly when wounded or offended, and continue, by faith, to embrace the wonderful world God has created for us.

Suffering (unfortunate but true).

Jesus stated in John 16:33 (specifically for his apostles, but it would fit for us as well) "in this world you will have troubles, but be happy, I have overcome the world (and in context, so have we in him). Suffering is a part of our life existence. We often marvel at suffering or rail against it as being so terribly unfair especially when we, or someone we love experiences it. Suffering and pain, which are part of the human condition, are only impactful in contrast to the wonderful blessings we have in Christ. This includes our ability to love, experience happiness and joy. Much of the character of a person can be seen in how they suffer…whether suffering embarrassment over a slight frustration, over a need not being met, or the more acute suffering caused by injury, loss, abuse, abandonment or betrayal.

The truth is, no one is exempt from suffering. We will not likely get out of this world alive, and we will all certainly share in the pain of being human. We can suffer with grace, but this is more easily said than done. It is possible, but only if we:

- Consider the source, which is rarely, except in the global sense, the devil or God, but life. Stuff happens in life, and our attitude should be less why me than why not me?

- Have courage. This simply means to have the willingness to feel the fear, feel the pain, not deny it, but do what you can each day to live life to its fullest. For some, it may be just getting out of bed.

- Recognize that some suffering, like the loss of a child, or horrible abuse cannot be accepted as just the way life is…outrage at injustice is also part of being fully human.

- Don't isolate yourself from the fellowship of the saints of God, or good friends and family in general. At the same time, you are not required to coddle fools; fools who say and do wrong headed things such as telling you God is teaching you a lesson. You may learn something from your suffering, but not from an insufferable buffoon. God has indeed provided us with a family, the family of God, who knows that God is good all the time, even when things go poorly.

As the Scriptures state, Jesus learned obedience thorough his suffering. He learned it in a most profound way, through the depths of his calling and purpose. He fulfilled his destiny as he embraced the fullness of his identity, as will we, which is the subject of our next chapter.

He is obviously having an identity crisis!

Chapter 3:

Identity — Who We Are

There are so many words that attempt to identify us. These begin with our gender, our personal name, and our specific physical and personality characteristics. Furthermore, there are many other names that identify our roles or functions. They include:

- American (or whatever), which identifies us as different from other cultures, with unique beliefs, ways of doing things, values, etc., which may or may not line up with biblical principles.
- Child, which we all are according to the word of God…God's children, but also we are someone's little boy or girl…at least to our mothers.
- Adult, this is to begin at age 18 [officially], though now days this seems to be delayed by several years.
- Wife or husband, mother or father, worker or Christian.

Only the last name (Christian) has the power to affect all other areas of identity. For to be a Christian, a true believer, requires a worldview that is distinctly different and infinitely richer than any other.

A World View is Key

A secular worldview suggests many different things. It is primarily self-oriented, materialistic, pluralistic, relativistic, pantheistic or atheistic (I won't define these terms for you…look them up!)

Much of this secular worldview or philosophical way of thinking is dramatically opposed to a Theo centric or Christ centric (God or Christ centered) worldview.

Our Christian Belief

A Christian belief system is based upon the historical facts of a personal and knowable God and his dealings with mankind. God, through Christ, created and continues to sustain the entire universe. He created all living things, including mankind, in his own image and likeness, so that we might rule over his creation. From the foundation of the world, the Trinity [Father, Son and Holy Spirit] knew that man could never live according to the holy standards of God. So, he made provision for man by sending himself, God the Son, to live and die for us. Through belief in the sacrificial death, burial and resurrection of Christ, we could experience the forgiveness of sin.

We can also experience the blessings of eternal life with God, and an abundant life, beginning now. Because of all that Christ has done, we can honestly proclaim, as affirmed by Paul the apostle, that when Christ died, we died with him. When he was buried, we were buried with him [symbolized in baptism], raised with him to resurrection life, and are now seated with him in the heavenlies. We are blessed to be a blessing. Being firm in our faith in all Christ has done for us, and believing all that scripture affirms about what we have received in Christ is true wisdom.

Still All about God...and Us

In our modern, post-Christian era, absolute truth is shunned. Anyone claiming absolute truth is labeled a fundamentalist, right-wing, Christian rightist, homophobic, charismatic fool; believing in psychics, ghosts, flying saucers, and reincarnation; no problem. I prefer a pre-suppositional view of scripture. That is, to assume that God is, not that we have to prove his existence by our intellectual acumen. There is ample evidence from science and logic to assume that the world, and we as humans, did not happen by accident, but by design. This does not prove that Jesus is the Christ, but to assume there is no God requires greater faith than I can muster.

Our Faith

Our faith in God is rational, and ultimately the most rational based upon historical facts and not some weird science. It is the only worldview that provides a safe harbor in the vicissitudes of life.

Personal Identity

Most people embrace the faith of their parents, or reject it completely. Most young people will process through what they can and cannot accept from mom and dad. Our true identity is rooted in our relationship with Christ, regardless of healthy or unhealthy parents and life experiences.

In Ephesians 1:4, the Word states,

> "Just as He chose us in Him before the foundation of the world, that we would be holy and blameless before Him."

We are the Father's Sons

Further, in Romans 8:14-16 it says,

> "For all who are led by the Spirit of God are sons of God, For you did not receive the spirit of slavery to fall back into fear, but you have received the spirit of adoption as sons, by whom we cry, Abba! Father! The Spirit himself bears witness with our spirit that we are children of God, and if children, then heirs-heirs of God and fellow heirs with Christ, provided we suffer with him in order that we many also be glorified with him."

What a wonderful promise, which is more reality than promise. For the word of God affirms that this is not something we strive for, although we do have to live it out. It is something we have inherited like a DNA of sorts, and all that the Lord wants from us is to live out our son ship. That is, to act as though we are what God says that we are. What more can we do?

"Who knows how far up we are? Raise your hands."

Chapter 4:

Living Life in the Wisdom of God by Intention with Discipline

To Accomplish Our Goals

To complete anything of worth like high school or college, it takes discipline. Discipline means the willingness to give up something for something of even greater or of more value.

Why Wait?

For instance, it takes discipline to delay the gratification of sexual fulfillment for the purity of marriage, and to give up short-term financial power for the long-term financial gain provided (at least potentially) by a university education.

Of course, for discipline to be effective it must be cultivated. Here are some key disciplines of great importance for you to consider.

Discipline of Prayer and Praise

Prayer is communication or communion with God. Communion with the Lord can be formal or informal (face towards God). Developing a prayer life is not difficult. The most important thing to do is to begin cultivating and developing a prayer habit. In most cases, we must start out small, perhaps a few minutes a day. As our intimacy with God grows, (remember, God is a person, and we can talk with him from our hearts…no fancy words are required) so will our time with him become more important and precious.

We can talk with God about anything and everything, but the real key is learning to listen to his voice. It sounds like yours, but it is filled with thoughts and wisdom beyond your pay grade or mine.

Of course, whenever we begin to draw closer to the Lord, our flesh and the devil will fight us. Thus, discipline is required!

Discipline of the Word of God

God's Word is precious. In Psalms 119:105, it states:

> "Your word is a lamp to my feet and a light to my path."

In II Timothy 3:16-17, the apostle Paul states,

> "All Scripture is inspired by God and profitable for teaching, for reproof, for correction, for training in righteousness; so that the man of God may be adequate, equipped for every good work."

More Word, More Maturity

Obvious to every Christian is the importance of reading (devotion) and studying God's Word. This too takes discipline. In the Word of God, we find the complete revelation of the truth.

Direct guidance for living life to its fullest, is provided within its pages. Thus, to study or not, is not the question. It is essential, and it starts with simply opening the book and beginning; a spiritual mentor is always helpful in this process.

Discipline of Relational Accountability

The apostle Paul admonished believers in the city of Ephesus that a part of growing up to maturity was learning to "speak the truth in love" (Ephesians 4:15). If you were a child raised in the church, you have no doubt heard many things you did not need to hear. Gossip, slander, rumor, sinful responses, etc., are rampant in the church. To learn the discipline of speaking the truth in love requires accountable relationships.

For example, if a friend begins to gossip, remind them of their commitment to speak the truth in love. This may be sufficient to cause them to rethink their course of action. If it is not enough, perhaps peacefully withdrawing from the conversation is best. One thing is for certain, what comes around goes around and you reap what you sow. Positive, loving and direct communication is a sign of both maturity and wisdom.

Accountability Leads to Healthy Decisions

Over the next (up to) 100 years or so, we will face many forks in the road. Each day, we must choose our responses to life. For example, who will you serve (Joshua 24:15)? Many people will pull on you for loyalty, but more than the church, pastor, or even family, you must set your heart on loyalty to God, and ultimately serve him as you serve others.

Who will you believe in (Isaiah 53:1)? When there are contradictions between colleagues, friends, family and bosses, we must remain grounded on the truth of God's word. If you read the papers to find answers for life, let alone watching Fox News at CNN, you can be easily swayed. Remember to trust in the Lord, he will never leave you or forsake you.

Do you want more love (Hebrews 12:6)? We all do of course, and the truth is that the more you love, the greater your capacity to love. Forgive quickly, care as much as you can, be generous to all you are able to be generous with, and let the love of Jesus spread in and through your heart.

Wisdom is the Thing

So seek wisdom, and in your seeking gain knowledge and understanding!

"We only have a few rules around here, but we really enforce them."

Chapter 5:

Walk in Wisdom: Choose the Right Gate

You might wonder what a gate has to do with wisdom. A gate was/is an entry point to a city, house, etc. To enter a gate one required permission from the keeper of the gate. The gatekeeper had the authority to open or close the gate...similar to a door.

Ancient Gates

One of the gates in ancient Israel leading into the city of Jerusalem was called wisdom. By God's grace, we must enter the gate of wisdom, for the one with the authority to open the gate is here, Christ in us, the hope of glory.

Apostolic Authority Releases the Grace to Open the Gate

Historically, the wisdom gate was named for one of Jacob's (praise) sons, Simeon, whose name means "to discern or to hear." It takes ears to hear and eyes to see to hear from God, to know good from evil, and to choose good.

Of course, we enter His gates with thanksgiving for all he has done for us. In fact, a grateful heart, in spite of life's circumstances, is an indicator of wisdom and maturity, and it leads to a more satisfying life. So, with thanksgiving and praise we agree with the Word of God. In James 1:5 we read,

> "But if any of you lacks wisdom, let him ask of God, who gives to all men generously and without reproach, and it will be given to him."

More Word, More Maturity

> "But let him ask in faith without doubting...."

Further, in James 3:13-17 we read,

> "Who among you is wise and understanding? Let him show by his good behavior his deeds in the gentleness of Wisdom. But if you have bitter jealousy and selfish ambition in your heart, do not be arrogant and so lie against the truth. This wisdom is not that which comes down from above, but is earthly, natural, and demonic. For where jealousy and selfish ambition exist there is disorder and every evil thing But the wisdom from above is first pure, then peaceable, gentle, reasonable, full of mercy, and good fruits, unwavering, without hypocrisy."

Remember, the fear of the Lord is the beginning of wisdom, but our wisdom is to grow from there.

Paul admonishes us in 1 Corinthians 1:18-25, 3:19, 2:4, 2:6, and 2:13,

- The wise of the world don't always show wisdom
- Consider the cross...for the world still sees the cross as a waste of a good teacher/prophet

[Jesus]…but they don't get what the plan was, for the cross is the very power of God for salvation.

More from Paul

The wisdom of the world is foolish, if contrary to the word of God. The wisdom of God is:

- Backed by power
- Works in any age
- Is the thing we must obtain

As we seek wisdom, we do so by entering the gate, or if you will the door, which is Christ, the door to the Father. We are the door to the Son, and through your anointed and appointed five-fold ministry gifts. They are the gates or doors to the Son and your son ship.

Remember, you have not received a spirit of slavery leading to fear again, but you have received a spirit of adoption as sons by which we cry out, 'Abba! Father!'" and in Galatians 4:5,

> "So that He might redeem those who were under the Law, that we might receive the adoption as sons."

The apostle Paul describes our identity in terms of adoption. As a Christian, you belong to God. He is your Father, your maker, your Lord and your King. You must make a decision regarding your adoption. You really cannot be somewhat Christian any more than you can be somewhat pregnant. Who are we? Who are you?

- A child of God, a Christian
- A Son of God

- The Bride of Christ

My prayer is that you will fully embrace your identity; your heritage. Rejoice in it. Express your identity through your own unique personality, in your own unique style, and enjoy the journey with the Lord. Our identity leads us towards achieving our true goals in life, an abundant life; because wisdom is the thing, seek wisdom.

Addendum

Expanded Definition

To follow are some additions to the definition above, provided for clarity and expansion.

A. **Adjective**

From the word chakam OT: 2450, "wise; skillful; practical." This word plus the noun chakemah and the verb "to be wise" signify an important element of the Old Testament religious point of view. Religious experience was not a routine, a ritual, or a faith experience. It was viewed as a mastery of the art of living in accordance with God's expectations. In their definition, the words "mastery" and "art" signify that wisdom was a process of attainment and not an accomplishment. The secular usage bears out the importance of these observations.

Chakam appears 132 times in the Hebrew Old Testament. It occurs most frequently in Job, Proverbs, and Ecclesiastes, for which reason these books are known as "wisdom literature." The first occurrence of chakam is in Genesis 41:8, "And it came to pass in the morning that his spirit was troubled; and he sent and called for all the magicians of Egypt, and all the wise men thereof, and Pharaoh told them his dream; but there was none that could interpret them unto Pharaoh."

The chakam in secular usage signified a man who was a "skillful" craftsman. The manufacturers of the objects belonging to the tabernacle were known to be wise, or experienced in their crafts (Exodus 36:4). Even the man who was skillful in making idols was recognized as a craftsman Isaiah 40:20; cf. Jeremiah 10:9. The reason for this is to be found in the man's skill, craftsmanship, and not in the object which was being manufactured. Those who were experienced in life were known as "wise," but their wisdom is not to be confused with the religious usage.

Cleverness and shrewdness characterized this type of wisdom. Amnon consulted Jonadab, who was known as a shrewd man 2 Samuel 13:3, and followed his plan of seducing his sister Tamar. Joab hired a "wise" woman to make David change his mind about Absalom 2 Samuel 14:2.

Based on the characterization of wisdom as a skill, a class of counselors known as "wise men" arose. They were to be found in Egypt in Genesis 41:8, in Babylon Jeremiah 50:35, in Tyre in Ezekiel 27:9, in Edom in Obad 8, and in Israel. In pagan cultures the "wise" man practiced magic and divination: "Then Pharaoh also called the wise men and the sorcerers: now the magicians of Egypt, they also did in like manner with their enchantments" Exodus 7:11; and "...that frustrates the tokens of the liars, and makes diviners mad; that turned wise men backward, and makes their knowledge foolish" Isaiah 44:25.

The religious sense of chakom excludes delusion, craftiness, shrewdness, and magic. God is the source of wisdom, as He is "wise." Yet he also is wise, and will bring evil, and will not call back his words, but will arise against the house of the evildoers, and against the help of them that work iniquity" Isaiah 31:2. The man or woman who fears God, lives in accordance with what God expects, and what is expected of him in a God-fearing society, is viewed as an integrated person. He is "wise" in that his manner of life projects the fear of God and the blessing of God rests upon him. Even as the craftsman is said to be skillful in his trade, the Old Testament chakam was learning and applying wisdom to every situation in life, and the degree in which he succeeded was a barometer of his progress on the road of wisdom.

The opposite of the chakam is the "fool" or wicked person, who stubbornly refuses counsel and depends on his own understanding, "For the turning away of the simple shall slay them, and the prosperity of fools shall destroy them" Proverbs 1:32; cf. Deuteronomy 32:5-6; Proverbs 3:35.

B. Noun.

chokmah OT:2451, "wisdom; experience; shrewdness." This word appears 141 times in the Old Testament. Like chakam, most occurrences of this word are in Job, Proverbs, and Ecclesiastes.

The chakam seeks after chokmah, "wisdom." Like chakam, the word chokmah can refer to technical skills or special abilities in fashioning something. The first occurrence of chokmah is in Exodus 28:3, "And thou shalt speak unto all that are wise hearted, whom I have filled with the spirit of wisdom, that they may make Aaron's garments to consecrate him, that he may minister unto me in the priest's office."

This first occurrence of the word in the Hebrew Bible bears this out as well as the description of the workers on the tabernacle. The artisan was considered to be endowed with special abilities given to him by God, "And he hath filled him with the spirit of God, in wisdom, in understanding, and in knowledge, and in all manner of workmanship" Exodus 35:31.

Chokmah is the knowledge and the ability to make the right choices at the opportune time. The consistency of making the right choice is an indication of maturity and development. The prerequisite for "wisdom" is the fear of the Lord. "The fear of the Lord is the beginning of knowledge, but fools despise wisdom and instruction" Proverbs 1:7. "Wisdom" is viewed as crying out for disciples who will do everything to pursue her Proverbs 1:20. The person who seeks chokmah diligently will receive understanding, "For the Lord giveth wisdom: out of his mouth cometh knowledge and understanding" Proverbs 2:6; he will benefit in his life by walking with God, "That thou mayest walk in the way of good men, and keep the paths of the righteous" Proverbs 2:20. The advantages of "wisdom" are many, "For length of days, and long life, and peace, shall they add to thee. Let not mercy and truth forsake thee, bind them about thy neck; write them upon the table of thine heart, so shalt thou find favor and good understanding in the sight of God and man" Proverbs 3:2-4. The prerequisite is a desire to follow and imitate God as He has revealed Himself in Jesus Christ. Without self-reliance and especially not in a spirit of pride. "A wise man will hear, and will increase learning; and a man of understanding shall attain unto wise counsels, to understand a proverb, and the interpretation; the words of the wise, and their dark sayings." The fear of the Lord is the beginning of knowledge but fools despise wisdom and instruction" Proverbs 1:5-7. The fruits of chokmah are many, and the Book of Proverbs describes the characters of the chakam and chokmah. In New Testament terms the fruits of "wisdom" are the same as the fruits of the Holy Spirit; cf. "But the fruit of the Spirit is love, joy, peace, long-suffering, gentleness, goodness, faith, meekness, temperance, against such there is no law." Galatians 5:22-23, "But the wisdom that is from above is first pure, then peaceable, gentle, and easy to be entreated, full of mercy and good fruits, without partiality, and without hypocrisy." And the fruit of righteousness is sown in peace of them that make peace" James 3:17-18.

The importance of "wisdom" explains why books were written about it. Songs were composed in celebration of "wisdom" Job 28. Even "wisdom" is personified in the Proverbs. Chokmah as a person stands for that divine perfection of "wisdom" which is manifest in God's creative acts. As a divine perfection, it is visible in God's creative acts, "Doth not wisdom cry, and understanding put forth her voice... I wisdom dwell with prudence, and find out knowledge of witty inventions.... The Lord possessed me in the beginning of his way, before his works of old.... Then I was by him, as one brought up with him: and I was daily his delight, rejoicing always before him.... Now therefore hearken unto me, O ye children: for blessed are they that keep my ways" Proverbs 8:1, 12,22,30,32.

The Septuagint translations are: sophos ("clever; skillful; experienced; wise; learned"); phronimos ("sensible; thoughtful; prudent; wise"); and sunetos ("intelligent; sagacious; wise"). The KJV gives these translations, "wise; wise man; cunning."

C. Verb.

Chakam OT: 2449, "to be wise, act wisely, make wise, show oneself wise." This root, which occurs 20 times in the Old Testament, appears in other Semitic languages, such as in the Akkadian word chakamu. The word means, "to be wise" in Proverbs 23:15, "My son, if thine heart be wise, my heart shall rejoice, even mine." In Psalms 119:98 chakam means, "to make wise." "Thou through thy commandments hast made me wiser than mine enemies, for they are ever with me."

(From Vine's Expository Dictionary of Biblical Words, Copyright (c) 1985, Thomas Nelson Publishers)

About the Author

Dr. Stan DeKoven is the founder and President of Vision International University and the International Training and Education Network, which are worldwide ministries operating in over 150 nations. Dr. DeKoven has several academic awards including the Bachelors in Psychology from San Diego State University, Masters in Counseling from Webster University, the Doctor of Philosophy in Counseling Psychology from the Professional School of Psychological studies, and the Doctor of Ministry degree from the Evangelical Theological Seminary.

Dr. DeKoven is a licensed Marriage and Family Therapist in the State of California and Certified School Psychologist, with many clinical and professional memberships in various nationally known associations. Further, Dr. DeKoven is the author of over 40 books in the fields of Counseling, Practical Ministry, Leadership and Biblical Studies. He travels extensively speaking at conferences and seminars, expanding Vision to the nations of the world. For more information, you may contact him at:

International Training and Education Network, Inc. and
Vision International University
1115 D Street
Ramona, CA 92065
(760) 789-4700
Fax. (760) 789-3023
www.vision.edu
www.booksbyvision.com

Other Books by Stan DeKoven

Addiction Counseling
Assessment of Human Needs
Crisis Counseling
Family Violence
Grief Relief
Healing Community
I Want to be Like You, Dad
Marriage and Family Life
Parenting on Purpose
Twelve Steps to Wholeness
40 Days to the Promise
Journey to Wholeness
The Bible in Counseling
From Hurt to Healed

To Order:
1-800-9-VISION
www.booksbyvision.com

www.ingramcontent.com/pod-product-compliance
Lightning Source LLC
Chambersburg PA
CBHW061514040426
42450CB00008B/1613